Emotional Intelligence 101: How to Carve a Duck

Denny Smith

Copyright © 2021, Denny Smith

All rights reserved.

ISBN: 9798728903963

DEDICATION

I dedicate this book to my wife and best friend, Pat. She is the glue that has held our family together and the one who has been supportive through thick and thin. I consider myself lucky.

It is also dedicated to our three sons: Kyle, Ryan, and Jason. What a joy they have been and continue to be. To observe their kindness and compassion for others and to see them continue to evolve as loving, caring young men is an ultimate source of pride and happiness for Pat and me. They are amazing.

Bob,

What a treat to know you. Many memories — Nots, Coaching. Life is Good

Doug

TABLE OF CONTENTS

	Acknowledgments	i
	How to Use This Book	ii
1	What Carving a Duck is All About	1
2	Emotional Intelligence	5
3	This Stuff Works	9
4	Achieving Mental Wellness	12
5	Awareness Precedes Change	19
6	Nourish Your Mind	22
7	Breaking the News	26
8	Become Your Own Best Coach	29
9	Wherever You Go, There You Are	33
10	Gratitude	38
11	Be a People Builder	42
12	Solution Consciousness	46
13	Positive Expectancy	51

14	Action	56
15	The Attitude Mechanism	60
16	The Power of Self-Talk	64
17	Keeping Your Self-Talk Positive	68
18	Vivid Imagination	74
19	Patience	78
20	Dealing with Upset People	82
21	How Can We Fix This	85
22	There is Another Way	86
23	The Natural Order of Things	88
24	Get Out of Judgment	91
25	Light a Single Candle	94
26	The Beginning	97
	Summary	100
	About The Author	101

ACKNOWLEDGMENTS

There are many people to thank, starting with our publishing consultant, technical wizard, cover designer, and head of encouragement, Tim Schmidt of Agency 511 in St. Cloud, Minnesota; our proofreader and grammarian, Dale Neuschwander; our friends at Unity Spiritual Center for their help and support; Michelle Anderson Schroeder for sharing her expertise as a counselor and social worker; and the number one cheerleader, my wife Pat, for her patience and her willingness to read and re-read excerpts when an opinion was needed.

How to Use This Book

Motivational speaker Charlie "Tremendous" Jones says that what you read will determine where you are five years from now.

This is a free country so you can do what you want but let me offer a few suggestions to maximize the benefits of reading *How to Carve a Duck*. The format of short little chapters provides daily doses of thought-provoking ideas in just a few minutes. I invite you to read the entire book in a relaxed and casual time frame, then revisit the content on a regular basis.

You might keep it by your bedstand and end your day with a shot of **P**ositive **M**ental **A**ttitude. You can read for a few minutes in the morning to jump start your day. You can keep it on your desk at work to stay on track mentally and emotionally. If you are a bathroom reader, this may be a good addition to that library.

Open the book at random and see what pops up. If the section you select doesn't turn your crank, randomly go to another page to see if that message resonates. The table of contents may trigger a particular topic that meets your need for today.

One of my friends established a habit of jump starting his morning by reading four pages of his favorite book, *The Four Agreements* by Don Ruiz. He is on his tenth year and 70th reading. I started the same practice with Deepak Chopra's *The Seven Spiritual Laws of Success*. I not only enjoy the daily uplift but feel the power of spaced repetition, the mother of all learning. Good free throw shooters practice shooting free throws every day. Positive people practice positivity every day. Make a commitment to read and re-read something that is meaningful to you. Digest just a few pages a day for six months and feel the impact.

You nourish your body daily. Do the same for your mind. You spend time each day grooming the hair on top of your head. Why not take a few minutes to groom what is going on inside your head and set a positive tone for the day? A string of positive todays leads to a lot of happy tomorrows.

Warranty

This book comes with a warranty. Well sort of. I am confident that practicing the principles discussed in *How to Carve a Duck* will yield amazing results, both on and off the job. I don't claim credit for the ideas. Like most speakers and authors, it is my job to gather information and share the good news with you. If you embrace the ideas and act on them, chances are good that you will reap substantial benefit. The kicker is this: YOU are the one who makes things happen. YOU are the one standing behind the warranty.

pages a day for six months and feel the impact.

You nourish your body daily. Do the same for your mind. You spend time each day grooming the hair on top of your head. Why not take a few minutes to groom what is going on inside your head and set a positive tone for the day? A string of positive todays leads to a lot of happy tomorrows.

Warranty

This book comes with a warranty. Well sort of. I am confident that practicing the principles discussed in *How to Carve a Duck* will yield amazing results, both on and off the job. I don't claim credit for the ideas. Like most speakers and authors, it is my job to gather information and share the good news with you. If you embrace the ideas and act on them, chances are good that you will reap substantial benefit. The kicker is this: YOU are the one who makes things happen. YOU are the one standing behind the warranty.

CHAPTER 1

WHAT IS CARVING A DUCK ALL ABOUT?

Ok, it's a strange title, but there is a method to our madness. When my father-in-law took up wood carving in his retirement, he carved a little duck that was pretty good. In fact, we still have it. One of his favorite jokes was to ask, "How do you carve a duck?" The answer is simple. Take a block of wood and carve away everything that *doesn't* look like a duck.

"What does that have to do with anything?" you might ask. So many times, when things aren't working in our life, we want to throw everything out and start over, when all we have to do is eliminate (carve away) one or two little shortcomings and we're back on track.

If you would like to develop more patience, every time you find yourself thinking or acting impatiently, carve it away and you are left with a calm and patient demeanor. If you would like a kind and understanding tone of voice, every time you catch yourself talking in harsh tones, carve it away and soon your tone of voice is habitually calm and approachable. If you would like to develop more confidence, every time you observe yourself thinking and behaving like an unconfident person, carve it away and replace it with self-assurance. As you practice stepping out of your comfort zone and acting like the confident person you are, it becomes a way of life.

Consider this. The perfect duck already exists within the block of wood. The artist skillfully whittles away everything that doesn't resemble a duck and perfection is manifested. So it is with you. Love, joy, patience, happiness, kindness, and so many other wonderful traits already exist within you.

EMOTIONAL INTELLIGENCE 101: *HOW TO CARVE A DUCK*

Like the artist, as you skillfully whittle away the little nuances that prevent you from being all that you can be, your perfection also begins to surface. The tools you need to be the kind of person you wish to become already reside within you. Isn't that a wonderful thought?

In these short little chapters of *How to Carve a Duck*, you will be reminded of time-tested ideas that will help you achieve self-mastery and make "personal positivity" a way of life. Like the game of golf, it's simple, but it's not easy. Take a little stick, hit a little ball into a little hole, and if you do that in four strokes you become a championship golfer. Is that simple or what? But those who play the game know that it is one of the most trying sports on the planet, demanding hours and hours of practice. It requires getting out of the rough after a bad shot, just like the game of life. It takes precision, patience, and emotional intelligence beyond the ordinary, just like the game of life.

Being patient, kind and accepting, using a calm and soothing tone of voice, treating people with respect and dignity—even when they may not deserve it—is also simple. It's just not very easy. But with practice, self-discipline, and desire, all these things are doable.

Your first task is to do some self-assessment to determine where you are, where you want to go, and what you want to achieve. On the next page, entitled "Carve Your Own Duck" is a listing of personal/professional skills and attributes. Rate yourself on a scale of one to 10, one being low and 10 being high. When you finish, connect the dots to make a line graph. What you see to the left of the line is where you are; what you see to the right of the line is your opportunity for growth.

Carve Your Own Duck

Below is a list of personal/professional skills and attributes. Rate yourself on a scale of one to 10, one being low and 10 being high.

	1	2	3	4	5	6	7	8	9	10
Patience	.	.	.	.	.	.	.	.	.	.
Confidence	.	.	.	.	.	.	.	.	.	.
Self-Control	.	.	.	.	.	.	.	.	.	.
Problem-solving skills	.	.	.	.	.	.	.	.	.	.
Staying calm under fire	.	.	.	.	.	.	.	.	.	.
Staying positive	.	.	.	.	.	.	.	.	.	.
Time management	.	.	.	.	.	.	.	.	.	.
Approachability	.	.	.	.	.	.	.	.	.	.
Tone of voice	.	.	.	.	.	.	.	.	.	.
Listening skills	.	.	.	.	.	.	.	.	.	.
Getting out of judgment	.	.	.	.	.	.	.	.	.	.
Creating a positive climate	.	.	.	.	.	.	.	.	.	.
_____	.	.	.	.	.	.	.	.	.	.
_____	.	.	.	.	.	.	.	.	.	.

Reflect for a few minutes on just one or two skills you will strive to master first, then practice the principles and techniques outlined in the book to achieve that mastery. You will go through your ups and downs but keep working at it. You don't have to tell anyone what you are doing, just be diligent and quietly go about your quest. I can guarantee that you will begin to feel the difference.

Here are some benchmarks to see if *How to Carve a Duck* is working. If you find ideas popping into your head occasionally, it is starting to work. If you find yourself acting on those ideas and making changes in the way you think and act, it is *really* starting to work. If people begin to notice your increased positivity and enthusiasm and say, "Whatever you're on, I want some too," *you have arrived.*

Nowhere is it written that we must have long faces and stern looks to enjoy life and achieve success, so make sure you're having a little fun along the way.

CHAPTER 2

EMOTIONAL INTELLIGENCE

Before we begin, let me share a message based on whether you are over or under middle age. (You decide what that is.) If you are under middle age, don't wait until you're in your sixties to learn this stuff—do it *now*. If you are over middle age, it is never too late to learn. I am at the age where I don't buy green bananas, but I have experienced more growth in the past two years than ever before. Had I learned this when I was 25, I could have avoided some of the pitfalls and would have enjoyed even more good than I have already been blessed with. So, let me remind you again—do it *now*—and attack it with joy and a sense of purpose.

Defining "Emotional Intelligence"

Emotional intelligence isn't an emotion, it's a *decision*. It's about teaching yourself to think before you act. When you make a conscious choice to be more patient, more confident, to maintain composure under fire or to trade a harsh tone of voice for a calm and more approachable one, you will be on your way to an ever-increasing level of self-mastery that will bring more joy, inner peace, and accomplishment than you ever imagined. Let's look at some formal definitions of this thing we call emotional intelligence:

1. **"The capacity to be aware of, control, and express one's emotions; and to handle interpersonal relationships judiciously and empathetically."**

This is good but it is a mouthful and academic, so let's simplify it a bit.

2. **"Skill in perceiving, understanding and managing emotions and feelings."**
   This is more precise and a little easier to digest, but there is a third that may be even simpler.
3. **"The ability to keep yourself under control, even when you don't want to."**
   In other words, you would like to punch their lights out, but you manage to keep your composure and respond with poise and self-assurance.

The first two I retrieved from the internet and there are literally hundreds available. I'm partial to the third one because it's kind of my own version and easy to understand. The point is this: It doesn't make any difference which definition you choose—just *use* whatever you subscribe to. Develop a strategy and apply it.

Achieving a high level of emotional intelligence is one of the surest ways to help you achieve success in any endeavor. Your career success, your relationships, and your effectiveness on any committee or in any leadership role are all buoyed by your ability to keep yourself under control.

The third definition talks about maintaining control, *even when you don't want to.* There is a simple measure of your desire. If you are improving and your determination to hold your cool is stronger than your willingness to fly off the handle, you are making significant progress, so chalk up the victory and realize that the power to keep yourself under control is yours to own. As you continue to practice, it will soon become your standard operating procedure.

How to Practice Emotional Intelligence

"Practicing" emotional intelligence may sound silly, but mastery of anything requires practice. You will hear this phrase often: *Awareness Precedes Change.* You create awareness by observing what you think and do and by monitoring how you respond to the world around you. Let me share a couple of personal examples.

Putting up outdoor Christmas decorations is not high on my "favorite things to do" list. Let me be more honest. I used to hate it and my wife, Pat, was often on the receiving end of my less than happy emotional state. Consequently, she often took the brunt of my frustration. Using a harsh tone, I would say things like, "Move the ladder on the other side of the bush," or "Hurry up. It's cold."

Three years ago, I knew that I was in a bad mood, so I disciplined myself to hold my cool and control my tongue. I got through the encounter without taking my frustration out on Pat and I felt pretty good about it. The next year I did the same and found the task less irritating.

Last year I actually enjoyed the experience and the time we shared together. It may seem like a small step, but I realized that self-control is possible and totally my own doing. The adage that every journey starts with a single step rang true. I'm not there yet, but the progress is rewarding, I am enjoying the ride, and I know it will transfer to other areas of my life.

The pandemic of 2020 curtailed our social life, but it did afford us more together time. We started playing a nightly game of 500 Rummy. Initially I dominated the win column, but then things went south. Pat started stomping me and I found myself using a lot of biblical terms, not in a biblical sense, if you know what I mean. Observing the ridiculousness of getting upset over a silly game of cards, I set a personal goal to curtail my frustration and I went to work. I'm doing well if I do say so myself, and the games are a lot more fun, win or lose. Don't get me wrong, I still like winning, but learning to detach from the outcomes reduces stress and increases enjoyment. Knock on wood, it's working.

In a later chapter on self-coaching, we emphasize that the key ingredient in increasing emotional intelligence or any other skill is *desire*, and there is a good way to measure that. Feeling yourself improving indicates that the desire is there. Falling short more than you should and making excuses for it sends a message that you need to intensify your commitment. So joyfully and intelligently increase your awareness, get to work, and see what happens. I think you'll like it.

CHAPTER 3

THIS STUFF WORKS

Before we get into the nuts and bolts of *How to Carve a Duck,* let me explain why I wrote it. I *know* this works because it's working for me, and if it's working for me, it can work for you.

The purpose of *How to Carve a Duck* is to introduce you to a powerful self-coaching tool kit that will help you become more patient and more confident, develop a kinder tone of voice, or master almost any emotional skill that you would choose to master. Applying these techniques will invite more career satisfaction, more enjoyable relationships, more peace of mind, and more happiness into your life. From personal experience, I *know* it works.

At my age I have more yesterdays than tomorrows, but as I mentioned earlier, I have had more growth in the past two years than at any time in my life and I'm still growing. I have to give credit to the fact that, with the help of many wonderful authors and mentors, I am teaching myself *How to Carve a Duck.* (Key phrase: "teaching myself"*)*

Let me illustrate. We have an organization in St. Cloud (MN), the Local Education Activities Foundation, that was founded to help fund athletics and other activities in our schools. Fifteen years ago I was asked to direct "Night of the Stars," a talent show that served as a fundraiser and showcased the talent of our students. Having spent 30 years as a "Type A" authoritarian basketball coach, I could give a pep talk with the best of them but when it came to dealing with problems, the "my way or the highway" mentality surfaced more often than it should have. My previous mentors and role models operated that way and they won championships, so much of my quest for success was influenced by that model. I was often impatient with the kids; many times I was short tempered and consequently was not always as cordial as I could have been. My lack of self-control often created a toxic climate, all excused by "the ends justify the means" mentality. Let me repeat, I was positive and inspiring most of the time, but staying calm under fire was not my strong suit.

"Night of the Stars" was highly successful. We had wonderful crowds and some standing ovations along the way, but in the early years I am sure my leadership style made the experience less enjoyable than it could have been for the students.

By observing and choosing different role models, I discovered that there is a better way. I found that I could get better results and enjoy a lot more success and happiness simply by altering my leadership style. By teaching myself *How to Carve a Duck,* I developed a self-coaching system that changed my attitudes and behavior in a remarkable way. As a result, I moved from being a "Screaming Mimi" to a calm, fun-loving and patient leader, which totally changed the climate and culture of the show. In my last two years as director, I didn't once raise my voice, so I know from experience that learning how to carve a duck gets some positive results.

You will notice a recurring theme throughout the book. At no time do we profess or expect perfection. I still blow it occasionally, but one of the cornerstones for the success of the process is to cut yourself some slack when you do. When you backslide, remind yourself that we're talking about progress, not perfection. You may not accomplish everything by the middle of next week and at times it may seem that you are taking some backward steps, but that's all a part of participating in this wonderful adventure we call life. Growth and change come in incremental steps, so recognize that and be intrigued by it.

Let's revisit some thoughts based on "over middle age/under middle age." Don't wait until you're in your sixties to learn this stuff, do it now. Mastery will propel you to new heights in both your career and personal life. For those of you who are at a more advanced stage of life, you can derive so much enjoyment as you grow through the remainder of your time on this wonderful ball of mud we call the earth.

Plain and simple, this has worked for literally thousands of people, it's working for me, and I know it can work for you. Go for it.

CHAPTER 4

ACHIEVING MENTAL WELLNESS

More than 40 years ago the term "wellness" began to appear in medical terminology. Prior to that, we talked about being sick or being healthy. The term "wellness" crept into our vocabulary and provided a new spin on the conversation. We can apply the same dialogue to a discussion of our mental well-being.

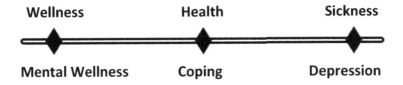

In the old days, if you weren't sick, you were considered to be "healthy." The move towards wellness triggered a more enlightened approach to physical well-being. Doing things that brought an optimum amount of energy and vitality became an avenue to living a rich, full, healthy life. Health clubs, spas, and fitness classes made their entrance on the scene. Today they are all over the place. Home fitness gear has become a booming business. Online and television fitness classes are readily available and fitness coaches are abundant. Healthy eating and nutrition programs are common television themes. Jogging, cycling, pickle ball, weight training and other fitness routines are a part of many people's regular routine and those who participate tout the benefits.

Let's revisit some thoughts based on "over middle age/under middle age." Don't wait until you're in your sixties to learn this stuff, do it now. Mastery will propel you to new heights in both your career and personal life. For those of you who are at a more advanced stage of life, you can derive so much enjoyment as you grow through the remainder of your time on this wonderful ball of mud we call the earth.

Plain and simple, this has worked for literally thousands of people, it's working for me, and I know it can work for you. Go for it.

CHAPTER 4

ACHIEVING MENTAL WELLNESS

More than 40 years ago the term "wellness" began to appear in medical terminology. Prior to that, we talked about being sick or being healthy. The term "wellness" crept into our vocabulary and provided a new spin on the conversation. We can apply the same dialogue to a discussion of our mental well-being.

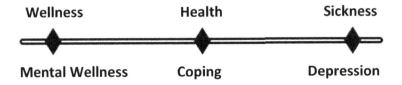

In the old days, if you weren't sick, you were considered to be "healthy." The move towards wellness triggered a more enlightened approach to physical well-being. Doing things that brought an optimum amount of energy and vitality became an avenue to living a rich, full, healthy life. Health clubs, spas, and fitness classes made their entrance on the scene. Today they are all over the place. Home fitness gear has become a booming business. Online and television fitness classes are readily available and fitness coaches are abundant. Healthy eating and nutrition programs are common television themes. Jogging, cycling, pickle ball, weight training and other fitness routines are a part of many people's regular routine and those who participate tout the benefits.

We can pay the same attention to our emotional state. On one end of the spectrum is depression and other forms of mental challenges. In the middle are those who are "coping." They say, "Hey I'm getting by, just leave me alone." Then there's the concept of "mental wellness," the ability to get as much kick out of life as possible and to live in a state of happiness most of the time.

There are so many similarities when comparing what it takes to achieve physical and mental wellness. If I told you that I had sore back, and a year later I still had a sore back, you might ask, "Have you seen a doctor?" If I answered "No," you would encourage me to seek professional help.

The same applies to mental and emotional challenges. If you have been struggling with depression or other emotional issues, seek professional help. There should be no more stigma attached to seeing a counselor for help with your emotional state than there is for seeing a medical doctor for a physical concern. Get the help you need and eliminate any trepidation you may have for doing so.

Two key ingredients required for physical wellness are diet and exercise. Those same ingredients can contribute to a healthy state of mind. What you feed your mind and the way you exercise control over your thoughts and attitudes are powerful determiners of your level of peace, serenity, happiness, and your overall emotional state.

Achieving wellness may require lifestyle changes, including a strong desire, a firm commitment, and a ton of self-discipline. Changes in your mental well-being may require changes in the way you think, the way you approach problems, and the way you deal with people. It is well documented that exercise and nutrition affect both your physical and emotional health. As hard as it may seem some days, discipline yourself to take care of that miraculous body you live in.

Alcohol is a depressant, so reducing or eliminating alcohol may be worth considering. That martini or scotch on the rocks may give you a temporary high but has adverse effects in the long run. If you are Debbie or Danny Downer more often than not, this is something to think about.

There are so many things you can choose to do to take responsibility for your emotional state if you have the will to do so. None of it is easy, and it may not happen immediately, but for most of us it is achievable. The motivational speakers remind us, "If it is to be, it is up to me."

The late Dr. Wayne Dyer said the greatest challenge in life is to learn to enjoy it. If *How to Carve a Duck* inspires you to make a commitment to achieving a higher level of inner peace, serenity, and happiness and introduces you to additional resources to help master that art, our mission will be accomplished.

Full and persistent commitment is paramount. W. H. Murray, the leader of the Scottish Himalayan Expedition, explains its power: "The moment one truly commits providence moves too, and all sorts of things begin to occur that would have never otherwise occurred." You will always experience peaks and valleys but with determined effort and a strong commitment, two things will happen. You will realize that when you are in a downer, you don't have to stay there—you can do something about it. Secondly, you will find that your times in the valley will be shorter, fewer, and farther in between. *How to Carve a Duck* is not meant to be the end-all answer to any issue, but to give the reader an opportunity to reflect on what is important and offer encouragement to pursue a plan to rise above the challenge.

Mental well-being is complex and more difficult for some to achieve than others. If you or someone you love are struggling, or if you just want to enhance the path you are on, there are so many great resources available. Some that have benefited me include Eckhart Tolle's *The Power of Now*, Deepak Chopra's *The Seven Spiritual Laws of Success*, and Chris Prentiss' *Zen and the Art of Happiness*. Candice Pert's *Molecules of Emotion* is very technical and is sometimes difficult to understand, but I was amazed at how much documentation there is to affirm the power of thought and its ability to heal our mind and body. These sources also allude to the importance of spiritual development and daily meditation.

For those of you who feel you are on track and want to maintain your emotional well-being, continue to grow because even a train that is on the right track will get run over if it doesn't keep moving.

In the Meantime, Do Something.

My first-ever sales manager shared a prayer that makes a lot of sense: "Lord, grant that someday I may do something right. In the meantime, grant that I may do something."

If you or a loved one is suffering from anxiety or depression, do something to break its hellish cycle. I claim no expertise on the subject, but I can share what I have learned from my personal challenge. One chapter of one book won't begin to scratch the surface of such a complex issue, but It can suggest that thousands of people have won the battle and have elevated themselves from a feeling of devastation to absolute happiness. Perhaps you can do the same. There are some minimal steps you can take to get started on your path.

The first, and perhaps most difficult, is to break the cycle of spiraling negativity. Muster every possible ounce of determination you can to conquer negative self-talk and get help if you need it but realize that the ultimate responsibility rests with you.

An attitude of gratitude is high on the list. The experts who advise being truly thankful for what you have and to hold tight to those things throughout the day number in the thousands. Did you sleep in a warm bed? Did the toilet flush? Do you appreciate your gift of sight? Do you hear the birds sing? (See Chapter 10.)

One of the most difficult steps is forgiveness, including forgiving yourself. Letting go of anger and bitterness is not easy, but so necessary. Get out of the past and live in the now. This is not easy, and it is not "one and done." About the time you think you have let go of a grudge or are over being angry, it can resurface, and you will have to start all over again. If you accept this as a part of the game and are willing to overcome hurt and anger again and again, you will return to a state of peace and contentment again and again. Eventually, recovery will be instantaneous, and a state of harmony will be yours, at least most of the time.

Our Optimist Creed advises to "forget the mistakes of the past and press on to the greater achievements of the future." Spiraling memories of past mistakes through your consciousness creates a devastating cycle of negativity. Do whatever it takes to break the cycle. I suggest reading pages 3 through 6 of Eckhart Tolle's *The Power of Now* and know that a path to happiness does exist. **If you believe it; you will find it**. I'm going to repeat that. **If you believe it; you will find it.** There is hope, and help is available. You don't have to go it alone. We talk about this in more detail in a later chapter, but this concept is so important that I want to interject it here as well. **You deserve to feel good about you.** Doubt about being deserving is a roadblock to happiness. I hope to convince you that you are worthy and deserving of all of the good that life has to offer. The core of your being, your very essence, is goodness.

The closing line of Bette Midler's *The Rose* perhaps best describes the wonder that lies within you.

> Just remember in the winter
> Far beneath the bitter snows
> Lies the seed that with the sun's love
> In the spring becomes the rose.

Mental Wellness:

The ability to get as much kick out of life as possible and to live in a state of happiness most of the time.

CHAPTER 5

AWARENESS PRECEDES CHANGE

This chapter is the foundation of everything we do from here on in. The ideas are deep, profound, and powerful.

Don't do it yet, but say to yourself, "I am going to move my arm." Now move your arm. You said "I" am going to move "my" arm, and your arm moved when commanded. Here is a deep question. Who is the "I" and who is the "my?" Who told your arm to move and who moved it? Are there two of you?

We have located the command center in the brain–the part that sent the message to your arm to move, but we have never located the "commander" of the command center. That's your higher self, your higher awareness, your higher consciousness, your oneness with the Universe, your observer, or whatever you choose to call it. Whatever you choose to call it, it is there; and therein lies your power as a human being. That power differentiates us from other forms of life. We can think about what we think about.

How to Carve a Duck is all about using your awareness to help you change anything that you wish to change and to attract the things into your life that you wish to attract.

So here's the key. *Be aware of your awareness.* And I did say "Be aware of your awareness," because "Awareness precedes change."

Be aware of what you are thinking and what are you doing and observe your emotional state right now. How are you responding to an upsetting situation? Are you reacting with anger and frustration, or are you consciously exercising self-control? What thoughts and experiences brought you to your current state of mind? Who or what are you judging right now? Are you looking for the wonderment in people or are you looking for their flaws? Do you notice and judge the unkempt person's long and scraggly hair, or do you see the miraculous human being living inside of that outer form? Are you aware of the colors and sounds around you? Are you enjoying the beauty of nature?

If your goal is to become more patient, your first step is to detect your impatience, then carve it away and make a conscious effort to replace impatience with control and calm. Patience is not as much an emotion as it is a decision, and we will repeat that often. Patience is not as much an emotion as it is a decision.

If you want to develop a kind and approachable tone of voice, monitor your current tone. If it is harsh, carve the harshness away and use a tone of voice that leads to open and civil discussion. If you find yourself wallowing in negativity and self-pity, be aware of it and know that you have the power to change. It's not easy to eliminate negative thinking, but if you are aware of it and realize the toll it takes on your happiness, you have taken the first step to changing it. *Awareness precedes change.*

The more mindful you are, the more peaceful and resourceful you become. The more aware you are of the absolute wonder of life and the opportunity you have every day to make a difference in the lives of the people around you, the more effective you become in everything you do.

Recall an idea from a previous chapter. The perfect duck already exists within the block of wood. All the carver has to do is shave away all the stuff that *doesn't* look like a duck. So it is with you. You are endowed with the perfection that already exists within you. Just carve away thoughts and behaviors contrary to that, and the perfect you begins to manifest. You are amazing and getting better every day.

EMOTIONAL INTELLIGENCE 101: *HOW TO CARVE A DUCK*

[I give credit to and thank the late Dr. Wayne Dyer for these ideas that have made a significant difference in my life. May he rest in peace.]

CHAPTER 6

NOURISH YOUR MIND

A little girl queried, "Daddy, sometimes I have positive thoughts going through my mind and at other times my thoughts are so negative. Why is that?" The father explained, "Well, on one shoulder you have a good wolf who is giving you all kinds of positive ideas; on the other shoulder is a bad wolf who is feeding you negativity. They are constantly fighting with each other." The little girl asked, "Which one is going to win?" The father replied, "It depends on which one you feed."

You are constantly bombarded with thoughts, some good and some not so good; some from the outside and some from the inside. You are always engaged in thought, so the question is this: Are your current thoughts feeding the good wolf or are you letting the outside world or your own negativity feed the bad wolf? Whichever one you feed is going to expand, so be careful and always be aware of what you are thinking. Earl Nightingale, one of our original and premier motivational speakers and the grandfather of audio learning, reminds us that "You become what you think about most of the time."

Let Me Sell You on One Idea

If someone were to say, "Look, I don't believe in this motivation stuff. Frankly, I think it's a bunch of fluff, but I will try one idea for 30 days. What would you suggest?" It would be this: Do something every day to program positive thoughts into your precious mind. Your body needs nutrition on a daily basis. So does your mind. Get in the habit of nourishing it every day.

Get up in the morning, pour a glass of juice or a cup of coffee and start your day by reading something positive. If you have not read Zig Ziglar's *See You at the Top*, I highly recommend that you do so. In the mid-80s I read a book by Dr. Gerald Jampolsky entitled *Love is Letting Go of Fear*. It began to change the way I was dealing with my athletes, it changed my parenting, it changed the way I looked at other human beings and it improved my outlook on life in general. The ideas expressed planted seeds that blossomed into powerful and pleasant changes in behavior.

Filling your mind with uplifting ideas yields a whole lot more joy and happiness than wallowing in negativity. You have within you, that little thing the size of half a grapefruit that we call the human brain, a mechanism that has power beyond our wildest imagination. Take time to nurture that wonderful goal achieving mechanism with good stuff every day. Read good books, listen to audio programs during drive time, make a concerted effort to keep yourself positive and upbeat, laugh a lot, and you will notice remarkable results.

This applies regardless of where you are in life. If you are in a downer right now, change what you are thinking, what you are doing, and the way you treat others and things will change accordingly. If you are at the top of your game, there is no limit to the amount of joy you can experience by continuing to nourish yourself with uplifting thoughts.

That Motivation Stuff Doesn't Last

Zig Ziglar was challenged by a seminar participant. "Zig, this motivation stuff is good, but it doesn't last. I go to seminars and I'm all fired up for a few days but then I'm right back down in the dumps." Zig replied, "Well of course. It's like taking a bath. Bathing doesn't last very long but it's a good habit to get into." That is precisely why you need to make reading uplifting material and listening to inspiring audio programs a regular routine. It requires constant attention.

Keeping yourself positive and dealing with life's ups and downs in a resourceful manner takes practice. You attend a seminar or read a book and get emotionally charged, but without doing something to keep the flame alive, the inspiration dissipates. When your hair gets messed up during the day you comb it. When your thinking gets messed up, take care of it. Keep feeding the good wolf.

For the next 30 days, when you get up in the morning and before drifting off to sleep at night, read something uplifting. Carve away negativity and focus on the pleasant events of the day. You will enjoy increased energy, enthusiasm, and peace of mind. Using the words of Mikey from a cereal commercial decades ago, "Try it. You'll like it."

That Motivation Stuff Is Like Taking A Bath. It Doesn't Last, But It's Still A Good Thing To Do.

CHAPTER 7

BREAKING THE NEWS

This is not a coincidence, but just after finishing Chapter 5, I saw a story on national television that clearly illustrates the power of the carve a duck concept and lays the groundwork for the rest of our journey.

A youth soccer referee got fed up with the behavior of parents. They were more than just yelling at the referees—they stormed the fields, violently attacking the officials and opposing parents, and even the kids. They threw punches, kicked each other, and shouted obscenities. It was abhorrent.

Many of the incidents were caught on video so one referee launched a campaign to spread the videos on social media. Although he may have been partially motivated to embarrass them, his major intent was to let them see themselves in action and do a little examination of conscience. It began to work. As the parents observed the ridiculousness of their less-than-fourth-grade emotional intelligence, they began to change.

One mother wrote to the referee to let him know that she had gone four weeks without yelling at an official. This is a perfect illustration of the carve a duck process. When she saw herself engaged in behavior that she didn't like, she carved it away and was left with a more civil and sportsmanlike approach to her child's youth soccer experience. Carve away the stuff that you don't like, and you are left with the perfect duck.

Here's a similar illustration. Television has been instrumental in changing coaches' sideline demeanor, especially at the college and professional levels. In the old authoritarian days, coaches would lose their tempers and vehemently berate their players during the game. But television caught them up-close and personal and let the whole world see them in action. It also provided a mirror for the coaches, and I am guessing that their initial thought may have been that they didn't want people to see them behaving like that, but then it went to the next level. They decided they didn't want to see *themselves* behaving that way, so they disciplined themselves to change. Carving away the displays of anger left them with a calm and collected bench and sideline coaching style which probably led to more success and a more enjoyable experience for their players.

You can apply this to any skill. Repeating our previous illustrations, if you want to be more patient, carve away impatience. When you observe yourself using a harsh tone of voice, get out of attack mode, settle down, and become calm and approachable.

Carving a duck involves three simple steps: Observe the way you think and act, decide what you want to change, then change. Mastery doesn't happen overnight. Like golf, or any other sport, it takes time and persistence, so strive for progress, not perfection.

One more golf analogy. All golfers make some bad shots and end up in the rough, but the good ones hold their composure, pull the right club out of the bag, and work themselves back onto the fairway. When you blow it—and you will—hold your composure, pull the right club out of the bag, and get back onto the fairway of life.

CHAPTER 8

BECOME YOUR OWN BEST COACH

Socrates once said, "All learning is self-learning." We all need teachers and mentors, but the reality is that you are the ultimate determiner of your thoughts and behavior. If you don't control your thoughts and behavior, they control you. So let's explore four steps to becoming your own best coach.

Desire

An old light bulb joke asks, "How many counselors does it take to change a light bulb?" The answer: "Only one, but the light build has to want to change." It illustrates the cornerstone for success in any endeavor—**desire**. Desire is paramount, and perhaps the most important element. Your desire to be non-judgmental must be stronger than your insistence on getting in the last zinger. Your desire to be confident must supersede your fear of getting out of your comfort zone and taking a risk.

If you want to exhibit more self-control, there is a way to measure your level of desire. Ask yourself if your ability to maintain control in upsetting situations is greater now than it was a year ago? If it is, you're making progress. If not, it may indicate that your desire needs to be cranked up, so rev up your determination, make a firm commitment, and mastery will follow. It boils down to this. "How bad do you want to be good?"

No Excuses

One of Dr. Wayne Dyer's last books was entitled *Excuses Be Gone*. As he conducted seminars on the topic, he would invite members of the audience to join him on stage for a coaching session. People would share horrendous experiences like abuse, addiction, childhood trauma, etc. Although he was empathetic and compassionate, he did hold their feet to the fire. He acknowledged the trauma and recognized that others may have caused them great harm, but he held them accountable for their own healing. He encouraged them to get the professional help they needed but emphasized that the ultimate responsibility to restore their mental health rested with them.

It is easy to carry a grudge and to wallow in anger and self-pity, and you may have every right to do so, but the outcomes of staying in that state of mind are unhappiness or even depression. You may have been wronged, you may have been treated unfairly, other people may have caused you harm, but the responsibility to heal rests squarely on your shoulders. This is an extremely difficult but necessary step to take if you want to achieve peace and serenity.

Eric Butterworth, one of my favorite authors, says there is a reason why you get upset. You get upset because you are upsettable. Those who challenge that idea might say, "You heard what that other person said, who wouldn't get upset?" or "My kids do some of the dumbest things. Of course I get upset." But Butterworth's assessment doesn't let you off the hook. You get upset because you are upsettable. No excuses.

My son, Kyle, is a self-taught computer whiz, starting in fifth grade in days of the old floppy discs. When something would go wrong, he would calmly ask, "Hmm. I wonder why it did that?" and used it as a learning experience as he calmly fixed the problem. His father was quite the opposite. One can only conclude from that scenario that I was upsettable, and Kyle was not. No excuses.

Monitor and Adjust.

Be your constant observer. When you feel yourself getting upset, observe (monitor) what you are thinking and what you are doing, then adjust and coach yourself into a resourceful state. Muster all the patience and emotional intelligence that you can and be accountable for your response. Tell yourself, "I can't control the way I feel right now, but I *can* control the way I think and act."

When you blow it, and you occasionally will, forgive yourself and move on. Mentally rehearse how you will handle similar situations in the future. Picture and visualize yourself reacting with patience and poise, and kindly say to yourself, "Hey, that's not like me. I am a patient, loving person and the next time I will conduct myself in a calm and confident manner." (We explore specifics of self-talk in later chapters.)

Practice, Practice, Practice.

This step is illustrated by the old joke about the guy in New York who jumped into a cab with his violin and asked, "How do I get to Carnegie Hall." The driver answered,

"Practice, practice, practice."

So-called "soft skills" are just that—they're skills. And like any other skills, they require practice. Mastering patience, self-control and emotional intelligence requires an extreme amount of practice. We don't often think of these things as skills, but they are. With attention to detail and persistence, they can be learned and honed like any other skill. So the next time somebody is getting under your skin and you feel yourself bristling up, say to yourself, "Gee, thanks. I have been working on becoming more patient, and you are giving me a wonderful opportunity to practice."

None of this stuff is easy, and mastery doesn't happen next week, which is why it is so important to engage in a life-long quest for personal growth and self-improvement. Take a few minutes each day to learn and grow and constantly nurture your emotional intelligence. Become your own best coach.

CHAPTER 9

WHEREVER YOU GO, THERE YOU ARE

When I first heard that phrase I thought it was kind of humorous, but reflecting on the hidden message, I found it to be profound. Let me illustrate.

A young couple just moving to a new town spotted an old codger sitting on a park bench, so they inquired about the people in their new place of residence. "What are people like in this town?" they asked. The codger answered their question with a question. "What were people like where you came from?" The couple replied, "They were kind of snooty, not friendly at all. It seemed hard to fit in, so it wasn't a lot of fun living there." The codger observed, "I imagine folks are pretty much the same here."

A second couple just moving into town made the same inquiry, "What are people like in this town?" The codger repeated the question he asked the previous couple. "What were people like where you came from?" "They were great," the couple replied. "They were warm, friendly and caring, and a lot of fun to be around." The codger echoed, "I imagine folks are pretty much the same here."

Many times we think that a change in job or location or career will solve our problems and sometimes that may be true. But if you seem to get the same results wherever you go, maybe it's time to alter the way you think, the way you act, and the way you inter-act with the people around you. Wherever you go, there you are.

EMOTIONAL INTELLIGENCE 101: *HOW TO CARVE A DUCK*

In my teaching days, if a student wanted to change classes because they didn't like the teacher, they had to get permission from both teachers before the switch was approved. One teacher, as a student was exiting her class for greener pastures, said, "Remember, you are taking you with you."

Sometimes change is just what the doctor ordered but be aware of the attitude and behavior you take with you when you make the switch. If you find yourself falling into the same trap over and over, look in the mirror and work on making you a better you.

When I was a junior in high school I got kicked out of band for disruptive behavior. A new teacher came in my senior year and I was allowed back in the fold. I gave a lot of credit to Mr. Root for providing a fun and rewarding musical experience, but I also know this: I came in with a whole new attitude and a whole new set of behaviors. Had I not changed, had I carried my former self into the new environment, there is a good chance the results may have been duplicated.

I have learned, sometimes the hard way, that if I carry anger, bitterness, worry, or any form of negativity with me, the results reflect that. When I approach any situation with enthusiasm, optimism, non-judgement, and all the good stuff, I elevate my chances for success. Success is wonderful, but the greatest benefit of a more positive approach is that you replace being stressed out and uptight with a relaxed feeling of peace and serenity. That's a pretty good trade.

Awareness Precedes Change

Let's revisit Chapter Five, *Awareness Precedes Change*. Before you can change anything, you must be aware of what you want to change. So *be aware of your awareness* by becoming your observer. Have a clear picture of the behavior you aspire to, monitor your thinking and behavior, then make the necessary adjustments. Our journey through *How to Carve a Duck* will arm you with the tools to achieve the demeanor you desire and make life worthwhile.

You're Good – But You're Getting Better

"I never make the same mistake twice. I make it five or six times so I know for sure things aren't working." It's one of my favorite one-liners that has a lot of meaning. Much of my frustration over the years has come from thinking that I needed to change other people or alter something "out there" to get the results I wanted. I eventually learned that if I changed myself and my approach, improved outcomes would follow. The adage, "If you always do what you've always done, you will always get what you always got," finally sank in.

Here's an important point. We don't have to approach personal growth and self-improvement from a standpoint of lack. You are already pretty good, but don't stop now. Zig Ziglar used to say, "I'm good—but I'm getting better." Approaching everything with that frame of mind makes the journey more rewarding and a whole lot more fun.

Keep coaching yourself to a resourceful state. Prepare to

take the most poised, positive, and enthusiastic you with you wherever you go and into whatever you do. Wherever you go, there you are.

Wherever You Go, There You Are.

CHAPTER 10

GRATITUDE

When I entered the speaking profession in 1978, I put together a 15-to-20-minute talk to give to service clubs to get started. I wanted to see what the motivators were saying about this business of attitude, so I began to research. I read books, I attended seminars, and I listened to audio tapes. (I'm dating myself here.) I found five common threads running through their messages. I formulated my first presentation cleverly entitled "Five Basic Attitudes."

At the top of the list was an attitude of gratitude. My favorite speaker, Zig Ziglar, said "The more you are thankful for what you have, the more you will have to be thankful for." Expressing gratitude focuses your precious energies on the positive and carves away negativity.

In 1999, at the tender age of 55, I went back into the classroom as a math teacher at Tech High School in St. Cloud, Minnesota. In 2010 I retired from teaching to re-enter the speaking profession, so I again researched what the speakers of the day were talking about. Almost everyone of them had gratitude at or near the top of their lists.

This is nothing new. Having a grateful heart is all over the Old Testament and a common thread running through most spiritual doctrines. I'm not pretending to be a biblical scholar but rather to illustrate that reference to a grateful heart has been around for a long time.

In a recent search of the internet, I googled "happiness." There are a countless testimonies from happy people explaining their joyful state and almost every one of them said they started and ended their day reflecting on what they were grateful for. Some kept a gratitude journal, others just mentally counted their blessings.

Gratitude doesn't require you to be grandiose. A friend in my congregation reminded us that common ordinary occurrences are worthy of recognition. The toilet flushed, the car started, you slept in a warm bed, the birds were singing. Reflecting on things that can easily be taken for granted cause us to say, "Wow." As you drive down the road in a car with thousands of moving parts all working together, marvel at how lucky you are to be warm in the winter and enjoy the coolness of the air conditioning in the summer. You have a choice of hundreds of radio stations. You turn a switch and the wipers clear your windshield. Amazing.

Review what you did in the last ten minutes. You finished an email, logged on to your computer, walked to the refrigerator and microwaved a snack, sat down at the table with a plate and utensils, listened to the music channel on TV while leisurely reading a newspaper, perhaps with the aid of bifocals. We can easily take things for granted, but to marvel at the wonder of little things heightens awareness of the beauty of creation.

The ultimate gift is life itself. You are one with the universe; with the trees, the stars, and all of nature. Life is a mixture of good days and bad days, but you can pat yourself on the back for this: Your success rate at getting through the bad days is 100%. That's a pretty good track record.

Being attentive to things you are grateful for also serves to quiet your racing mind. The basic premise of Eckhart Tolle's writing is that the ability to tame your inner dialogue leads to euphoric peace and serenity. Appreciating the beauty of your surroundings can help get you to that desired state. Dr. Wayne Dyer said that if you were limited to only one simple prayer he would recommend this: "Thank You. Thank You. Thank You."

If you are so inclined, put the book aside for a few minutes, close your eyes, take a few deep breaths, and remind yourself how lucky you are to be living in this moment. Life is a banquet, why bring a sandwich?

Life is a banquet. Why bring a sandwich?

CHAPTER 11

BE A PEOPLE BUILDER

I grew up in Morton, Minnesota. I know there are a lot of authors who claim they grew up in Morton, Minnesota, but I actually did.

It was a little town of 750 people, but I wouldn't trade growing up there for the world. We didn't have any amenities of a bigger city—no movie theatre, no bowling alley, no full-time fire department, just a group of volunteers. I'm not putting them down, they were good. We had a night club burning down outside of town one night and our department went out to fight it. Normally it would have burned to the ground by 10 o'clock at night, but our guys kept it going until 4:30 in the morning.

What I learned from living in a little town is that life is all about people. It's about how we get along, how we help each other, how we support each other. Now we live in St. Cloud, Minnesota, an area of about 100,000 people and do you know something? Living is St. Cloud is the same; it's all about people. It's about how we get along, how we help each other, how we support each other.

I have had the opportunity to speak in some of the larger cities throughout the country and I remember wondering what the big city folks would think of my message. I found that life in the big city is all the same; it's all about people. It's about how we get along, how we help each other, how we support each other.

A lot of speakers in a lot of different ways have said, "To the extent you help others get what they want do you get what you want." This is an absolute axiom of career success. A business thrives by serving people. We all want a good product at a fair price, but we also want employees to smile and be friendly and to show us they care. Good teachers and coaches know that they achieve their success by helping their students learn and grow. A supervisor becomes effective by helping his or her team members become effective. Those who bring more love *to* their relationships receive more love *from* their relationships.

One key to people building is to recognize the dignity of every person you come in contact with. We do that when we hold a baby. We marvel at that little miracle with eyes that see and a heart that beats, with hopes and fears and joys and dreams, and we do everything we can to make that little human being feel loved and warm and important.

Somehow we forget that as that little human being grows through life, it's still that same miracle. That eighth grader in your neighborhood with green spiked hair is still that miracle. The bus driver, the attendant at the gas station, the person on the committee that you don't see eye-to-eye with are all that same miraculous creation we call a human being.

You're in line at the grocery store and the elderly person in front of the line is confused and having a hard time counting change. It's easy to stand in the back of the line and impatiently think, "Hey, c'mon up there. I have places to go and people to see. Hurry it up." But stop. Stop and realize that inside of that outer form is still that living, breathing miracle. Still with eyes that see and a heart that beats, still with hopes and fears and joys and dreams, and still waiting for you to come along to make them feel loved and warm and important.

Here's the beauty of that kind of thinking: If you see the miraculousness in every human being you encounter, you can only make one conclusion about yourself. You must be that same miracle just the way you are. Isn't that a wonderful thought?

Earl Nightingale said, "The primary function of any organization is to make life more meaningful for others." What a great philosophy for a business to embrace, and it's one that we can all subscribe to individually as well. When you get up in the morning, focus your energies on making life more meaningful for your family or those you live with. When you leave for work, remind yourself that your primary focus is to make the day more pleasant and meaningful for the people around you. A smile to the clerk at the grocery store adds meaning to his or her life. A pat on the back to the kid in your neighborhood who doesn't get too many pats on the back means so much. A word of encouragement to your friend going through some tough times right now gives hope and a spark of optimism. As you practice making life more meaningful for others you find that you are the biggest beneficiary of your warmth and positivity. As you help others get what they want, you receive what you want.

Your Life is an Echo

A little girl was in an argument with her mother and realized that the wrath of mom was coming down upon her, so she ran out the back door shouting, "I hate you. I hate you. I hate you." Their home overlooked a valley, so the echo came back, "I hate you. I hate you. I hate you." Frightened, she ran back into the house and told her mom, "There is a mean little girl out there who says she hates me." In all her wisdom, the mother said, "There's another little girl out there and she's a nice girl. Why don't you go out and tell her that you love her? The girl overlooked the valley and shouted, "I love you. I love you," and the echo came back, "I love you. I love you."

Your life is an echo, and what you send out to others is coming back to you. You've been in the game of life long enough to know that you have to play the percentages on this one. Regardless of how well you treat some people, they will never return the favor. For the most part, however, the good you send out to others is coming back to you.

Being a people builder and making a habit of doing little things for others has side effects that include lower blood pressure, less anxiety, more peace of mind, being more fun to be around. These are side-effects you can live with.

CHAPTER 12

SOLUTION CONSCIOUSNESS

There are three things you can count on: water is wet, rocks are hard, and you will face problems today.

When the motivational speakers tout the benefits of positivity, we think "Oh, I get it. All I have to do is turn this little crank in my think machine and my problems go away, right?" That's not the case. You will face challenges every single day of your life, so the goal is not to eliminate problems, but to learn to deal with them in an emotionally intelligent manner and to recognize that it is not the problem that gives you the headache, but your attitude towards the problem that gives you the headache. Or as a speaker friend of mine, the late Mike Patrick used to say, "The problem is not the issue. The issue is how you deal with the problem."

Mike inspired thousands with his story. "In high school, I had the world by the tail. I was a good student, National Honor Society, a good athlete. I was relatively good looking; I got a date every once in a while." But the first football game of his junior year he went to make a tackle and the running back's knee pad caught his face mask and jerked his neck. He had some use of his hands and arms but was paralyzed from the chest down. When Mike looked at you from his wheelchair and said, "Folks, the problem is not the issue. The issue is how you deal with the problem," you knew he was coming from the heart.

EMOTIONAL INTELLIGENCE 101: *HOW TO CARVE A DUCK*

I can't begin to imagine what he went through. One day the band was playing, the crowd was cheering, there were college scouts in the stands wanting to recruit him, and the next day–in fact for the next 99 days–he was in the hospital in Sioux Falls being flipped upside down every 30 minutes so he wouldn't develop bed sores.

He had a lot of support. His mother was with him every one of those 99 days. The students from his high school in Worthington, Minnesota visited him. The band came to hospital and played the school song. His father encouraged him to go to college. Mike, however, knew that overcoming the challenges he was about to face was ultimately up to him.

He talked about speaking to a group of high school students and after the speech a young girl, down on her luck at the time and not very well groomed, shared her story. Mike encouraged her to have hope, to believe in herself, and to realize that with the right attitude and a lot of determination, she could overcome the obstacles she faced. A few years later he was speaking at a Community College and a young woman, neatly dressed and oozing with confidence, approached him and said, "Do remember when you spoke at such and such a high school a few years ago?" Mike said, "Yeah, I remember that." She continued, "Do you remember the student that talked to you after the speech, and you gave her a pep talk about believing in herself and changing her thinking?" Mike replied, "Yeah, I remember that." She said, "I'm that girl."

Mike's words inspired her to reframe her thinking, he

encouraged her to believe in herself and gave her hope for her future. So when your current problems seem insurmountable, reflect on Mike's insight. "The problem is not the issue. The Issue is how you deal with the problem."

Tangled Christmas Tree Lights

You can tell a lot about a person by the way he or she handles three things:

A rainy Day
Lost luggage
Tangled Christmas tree lights

One of my former ball players sent me that and the timing was perfect. We were about to take the tree down and my history of untangling the lights was not pleasant. I would get frustrated and my family knew it was time to back off and leave me alone in my misery. Reflecting on the quote, I decided to stay calm and do the job without getting visibly upset. It took me 15 minutes. In previous years it took the same 15 minutes, so the difference wasn't in the time spent, but in emotional control. The moral of the story is this: Life is a series of tangled Christmas tree lights. Untangle them.

Steps to Solution Consciousness

As the title "Solution Consciousness" suggests, the first step is to direct your mental energies away from the problem and focus on the solution. Clearly identifying the problem at hand is a necessity, but once that is achieved, direct your time and energy towards your desired outcomes. This is so obvious, but how many times do we find ourselves wasting precious emotional energy fretting over the problem instead of using our initiative, creativity, and talent to achieve a successful resolution? Albert Einstein reminds us that we cannot solve problems with the same consciousness that created them.

The second step is to spend less time fixing the blame for the problem and more time fixing the problem. (See Chapter 21: "How Can We Fix This?")

The third and most challenging is to keep yourself positive and in a resourceful state. Harlan Sanders, better known as the Colonel, had a successful restaurant business. But in his 70s they moved the highway seven miles away and the business folded. He took stock of what he could do and decided to sell other people in the restaurant business on the idea of selling his recipe. He became a millionaire and created other millionaires along the way. From the experience he coined the phrase, "Behind every problem is a bigger and better opportunity if you can only find the solution to the problem." As hard as it may seem, muster all the optimism you can, believe in yourself, tap into your God-given talent and, and keep on keeping on. As you forge ahead, heed Mike Patrick's words: "The problem is not the issue. The Issue is how you deal with the problem."

EMOTIONAL INTELLIGENCE 101: *HOW TO CARVE A DUCK*

The problem is not the issue. The issue is how you deal with the problem.

CHAPTER 13

POSITIVE EXPECTANCY

There are two components of positive expectancy. The first is the idea that you deserve to feel good about you. We have not always been taught that, especially people my age. When we got old enough to walk and talk, they told us to sit down and shut up. When we receive a compliment on the outfit we're wearing, we have a tendency to say, "Oh this has been in the closet for years," instead of graciously accepting the compliment with a simple "Thank You."

Frank Lapine, a gentleman in my hometown of Morton, told the Minister on his way out of church, "Pastor, that was a good sermon." The pastor smiled and replied, "Well, it was just God working through me." Frank replied, "Well it wasn't that good." The moral of the story is to graciously accept recognition and realize that it is OK to feel good about yourself. If you do want to share credit with others say something like, "There were a lot of others involved, but thank you. I really appreciate your kind words."

Dr. Wayne Dyer suggests having a quiet love affair with yourself. Not an arrogant "I am the greatest" mentality, but a genuine recognition of yourself as being loving, caring, and deserving. As we pointed out in Chapter 11, you are a miracle just the way you are. That is not arrogance, but a simple recognition of your miraculousness as a human being. You can totally believe in yourself and remain humble if you accept the definition of humility from one of my early seminar participants. "Humility is the realization that you are no better or no less than anyone else. We are all miracles."

If you struggle with feeling good about yourself, try this on for size. The days you feel good about you are the days it is easier to be more patient with others, or to listen to the coworker who really needs someone to be there for them, or to be kind to others. You are in a good mental frame to lift others when you are accepting of yourself.

2000 years ago, a guy told us to "love your neighbor as yourself." For the most part that's what we do. When we are in a state of being OK with ourselves, we show kindness to others. It is more difficult to show compassion and acceptance of others when we are down on ourselves. So, for your own good, and for the benefit of those around you, go ahead and have a quiet love affair with yourself.

The second component of positive expectancy is that you get out of life what you expect. If you are expecting joy, harmony, and success, you will attract those things to you. If you anticipate resolution to the challenges you face today, you greatly increase your chances to achieve that resolution. Writings like "The Secret" and "Law of Attraction" are so often misconstrued. We initially think that if I sit on my couch and affirm, "I will make a million dollars," money appears out of the blue, but the major premise is that your thoughts, both positive and negative, are powerful forces in attracting things to you. To repeat the words of authors like Henry David Thoreau, Earl Nightingale, Denis Waitley and so many others, "You become what you think about most of the time." The words "most of the time" are significant. We all encounter occasional bouts of negativity, but you have the power to keep those times to a minimum and redirect your thoughts in a positive direction, attracting to you the things that make life meaningful.

Science supports this. You have at the base of your brain a net-like group of cells called the *reticular activation system*, whose job it is to filter out unwanted information and allow desired information to go through. Buy a red sedan and you will be surprised at the number of red sedans you notice, especially when you can't find your car in the parking lot. A nun in one of my seminars who was being transferred to Redwood Falls, MN, said she had never heard of it until her relocation was imminent, then it started popping up all over the place. Redwood Falls had been in the weather reports for years, but she never noticed it until her awareness was heightened by her reticular activation system. (For the record, Redwood Falls is right next to my hometown of Morton.)

So why not direct your reticular activation system to seek the things you want instead of allowing negativity to channel it to attract what you don't want? Why not point your mental energies towards solutions rather than problems? You can think thoughts of love and harmony and gravitate towards love and harmony, or you can allow anger and frustration and other negative thought patterns to attract those things into your life. It is up to your higher self or your observer or whatever you want to call it to become aware of what you are thinking and what you are doing, but it's your job, through your awareness, to direct your thoughts and actions towards your desired outcomes.

Abracadabra

When we hear "abracadabra," we often picture magicians dazzling us with their sleight of hand tricks. Its origin, however, comes from Hebrew scriptures and sums up the power of the words you think and speak. *"It will be created by my words."* Be careful, because what you say is what you get.

Winston Churchill, known for his eternal optimism, said, "Pessimists see a problem in every opportunity. Optimists see an opportunity in every problem….I'm an optimist. Nothing else makes much sense."

Pessimists see a problem in every opportunity. Optimists see an opportunity in every problem.

CHAPTER 14

ACTION

This is an old joke, but I'm going to tell it anyway. There was an old run-down farm for sale in western Stearns County that nobody would buy because everyone saw it as dilapidated and useless. But one couple saw the farm not as it was but had a vision of the farm the way it could be. Bobby Kennedy summed that up nicely when he said, "Some people see the world as it is and ask, 'Why?' Others see the world as it could be and ask, 'Why Not?'"

With that attitude the couple bought the farm and for the next three years worked their fingers to the bone until they did indeed have one of the most beautiful farm sites in the county. Then the minister, with hands folded prayerfully, came to visit and said, "The Lord has blessed you with a wonderful farm." The couple replied, "You're right reverend, but we pooled our resources on the project. You should have seen this place three years ago when he farmed it all by himself."

That's not the funniest joke in my repertoire but it has a great message, pointing out two things necessary for success in anything you do. First you need a vision, a clear-cut picture of what you want to accomplish, then you need to take action to make the dream come true. Nothing happens until you carry out your intentions.

Action is the cornerstone of *How to Carve a Duck,* and hopefully that message resonates throughout the book.

Another repetitive theme is that change takes time and a willingness to persist until the goal is achieved. Mastery doesn't mean that you never slip up, but that you make consistent progress. Growth is incremental and sometimes painstakingly slow, so stick with it and give yourself credit for improvement. When you do notice improvement, give yourself a pat on the back and feel good about your accomplishment. You might even affirm, "Every day and in every way, I am getting better and better and better."

Someday Isle

We all take trips to "Someday Isle," that vacation resort that says, "Someday, I'll do that." A lot of motivational speakers criticize that mentality, but I think there is a significant place for it because it plants a seed for something you may pursue when the timing is right. "Someday I'll go back to college," or "Someday I'll take a computer class," or "Someday I'll do whatever." You have ignited a spark in your subconscious that may turn into a burning desire one day down the road.

I might suggest that you not procrastinate on honing your attitudes, emotional intelligence, or people skills, however. Work on those now, and while you are at it, decide to make it a lifelong quest.

Satori

The Zen Buddhist term "satori" means "instant awakening" or "instant enlightenment." What seems to be "instant" may not be instant at all. Liken it to a concept in chemistry. You remember (of course you do) from your high school chemistry classes that an atom has electrons orbiting the outer rings and a nucleus containing protons and neutrons and croutons. You also learned that when electrons rev up enough speed, they jump to the next ring in what appears to be an instant burst of energy. I have been told that in reality, the electron has been accelerating for a period of time until it gathers enough speed to make the jump. In short, something that appears to be instantaneous isn't instantaneous at all, but a culmination of momentum over time.

That is analogous to our quest for growth. It seems that one day we wake up with patience or a calm tone of voice and have a "satori," when in actuality we have been making steady progress for a period of time until the consistent effort pays off.

So don't get discouraged or lose sight of your goal when you backslide a little bit. If you take two steps forward and one step back, you are one step ahead of where you began. Do that each month for a year and you are 12 steps ahead of where you were when you started. Because the change is slow you may not notice it, but it is unfolding in marvelous fashion.

Keep your eyes on the prize and remember that the two basic requirements for success in any endeavor are vision and action. Clearly picture and visualize the behavior and mindset you aspire to, then do what it takes to make it happen. Add determination and a willingness to assume personal responsibility and success is inevitable.

When all the words were said and done
And all had been debated,
"The bottom line is attitude,"
The motivator stated.
The quiet man across the hall said,
"Sir, I disagree.
The bottom line isn't attitude,
That's the top line, don't you see."

For it's attitude that brings us to
Our good or bad attraction,
But the bottom line has always been,
And always will be *action.*

CHAPTER 15

THE ATTITUDE MECHANISM

When I ask my seminar participants "How Important are Attitudes?" I invariably get back short answers: "Very." "Critical." "Attitudes are everything." I believe that most of us subscribe to the fact that attitudes are an important part of our existence and if that's the case, it may benefit us to look at how the attitude mechanism works.

Think ----------

    Attitudes----------

        Behavior----------

            Results

The way you *think* determines your attitudes. Attitudes are nothing more than "habits of thought." Your *attitudes* determine your *behavior,* and your behavior determines the *results* that you get out of life. **It all starts with the way you choose to think.**

Let me illustrate. I do a lot of driving in my business and make frequent trips to Minneapolis, which is legally about an hour and a half from my home in St. Cloud. What if coming home from Minneapolis I trap myself into a negative thought pattern about my wife, Pat, and our relationship? "That little tiff we had last night. If she ever brings that up again, I'm going to tell her in no uncertain terms what I think of that. I'm out here beating the streets and she says something like that. Good gravy. And If she had done something different five years ago our life sure would be different now."

If I would think like that for an hour and a half, by the time I would get home my attitudes would be pretty lousy, my behavior would be cordial at best, and the results would probably not be very good. What if, on the other hand, I chose to think about the love we've shared for 52 years, or the joy we had in raising our family, or how when I needed her she was there for me all the way. If I would think like that for an hour and a half, by the time I would get home my attitudes would be a whole lot different, my behavior would be a whole lot different, and the results would be a whole lot different. Let me ask you this: "What changed?" The only thing that changed in those two scenarios was what I chose to think about, but what a dramatic difference in results.

We saw that work over an hour and a half. Multiply that by five, ten, fifteen, or twenty years and you can see that relationships are built on what we choose to think about, careers are built on what we choose to think about, and to a great extent, our lives are determined by what we choose to think about. To repeat a quote from Chapter 13, "You become what you think about most of the time."

The message in Chapter 6 on nourishing your mind is paramount. Start each day by reading something positive.

End your day with reflection on positive thoughts, including gratitude. Constantly observe your thoughts and behavior and redirect negativity towards a focus on the good that surrounds you. Taking control of your thinking is perhaps the surest way to take control of your destiny.

When you detect negativity, *carve it away* and clear a path for positive thoughts to abound. Keep yourself in a resourceful state. Read, listen to positive podcasts, take time for quiet meditation, laugh, take a leisurely walk as you marvel at the beauty of nature, exercise, have lunch with a positive friend, just to name a few.

Positivity isn't just a state of mind, it's a *decision.* Just for today, decide to be optimistic. Nothing else makes much sense. Stay mindful of the key phrase in this chapter: **It all starts with the way you choose to think.**

It All Starts with the Way You Choose to Think.

CHAPTER 16

THE POWER OF SELF-TALK

A little boy was in the middle of a tantrum at the store and his father said, "Henry, settle down. We're almost done, then we can go home." The boy's behavior continued in the next aisle and the father softly repeated, "Henry, just be patient. We can go pretty soon." A third time, the father, in a calming voice, said, "Henry, just a few more minutes, then we're going home." A fellow shopper, so impressed with the father's calm and soothing manner commented, "You were so patient with little Henry." The father replied, "*I'm* Henry. He's Steve. I was talking to myself."

When I ask my seminar participants how many of them talk to themselves, most of them raise their hand or nod their head, but not all. At breaktime during one session, a participant said, "When you asked that question, I sat back here thinking, 'This guy is nuts. I don't talk --- to --- myself.' I suddenly realized that I am always engaged in self-talk.'"

If you agree that you do indeed talk to yourself, we need to address a couple of follow up questions. Do you argue with yourself? If you don't think you do, try this. Stand in front of the mirror some morning and give yourself a little pep talk. Say something like "You are a kind, patient, loving person," and listen to what the voices inside of you have to say. I call them "little twerps," because they are nothing more than that unless you relinquish power to them. My twerps would say something like, "What do mean you are kind and loving. Do you remember when you were a sophomore in high school how you teased Denny Sullivan? You made him feel terrible. And don't tell me you are patient. I heard you screaming at your kids just the other day."

The third question is the most important. Do you win the argument? Whoever wins the argument between you and your twerps determines your attitude, your confidence, your self-esteem, and perhaps even your level of happiness. As simple as it may seem, being the master of your inner dialogue is not an easy task, but it is ultimately important and well worth putting time and energy into. What you say after "I am" is critical and an unbelievably powerful force in your life. "I am such an idiot," paints a whole different picture than "I am a kind and caring person." Both, however, do paint a picture.

Your Subconscious Mind

In our wildest imagination we cannot begin to fathom the power of the human mind, but let's take a surface look at its workings. Two major components are the conscious mind, the part of the mind that you think with, and the subconscious mind. The subconscious mind is a goal achieving mechanism that behaves much like a computer. A computer is given information, then responds to that information without judgement. For example, a bank employee programmed the bank's computer to take ten cents out of everyone's checking account and put it into his own. The computer made no value judgement. It didn't say

"Thou shalt not steal," or "Are you sure you want to do this? You may get caught." It just did what the programmer told it to do without judgement.

So it is with your subconscious mind. Every thought, every experience you have had is indelibly etched in the memory bank of your subconscious mind, never to be erased. The time you made the winning free throw in the big game, the time you starred in the high school musical, all of your successes are there. Unfortunately, so are the less pleasant incidents. The time you walked across your neighbor's lawn and got scolded, the time you made a fool of yourself at the school dance, the time you failed your Algebra II test. They are also etched in the memory bank of your subconscious mind.

If you feed yourself thoughts like, "I'm such a dummy," or "You never do anything right," your subconscious mind doesn't judge, it simply adds the information to its memory bank.

The workings of the human mind are so complicated and complex, and volumes have been written about its power, so one chapter of one book will not even scratch the surface of the available knowledge, but let's look at a few simple steps you can take to achieve mastery of your thoughts.

The first step, a theme we have emphasized often, is to create an awareness of what you are thinking and what you are doing. Awareness precedes change. Constantly monitor and adjust your thoughts. When you find yourself wallowing in negativity, carve it away and focus on something positive. Eckhart Tolle, in *The Power of Now*, kind and loving. Do you remember when you were a sophomore in high school how you teased Denny Sullivan? You made him feel terrible. And don't tell me you are patient. I heard you screaming at your kids just the other day."

The third question is the most important. Do you win the argument? Whoever wins the argument between you and your twerps determines your attitude, your confidence, your self-esteem, and perhaps even your level of happiness. As simple as it may seem, being the master of your inner dialogue is not an easy task, but it is ultimately important and well worth putting time and energy into. What you say after "I am" is critical and an unbelievably powerful force in your life. "I am such an idiot," paints a whole different picture than "I am a kind and caring person." Both, however, do paint a picture.

Your Subconscious Mind

In our wildest imagination we cannot begin to fathom the power of the human mind, but let's take a surface look at its workings. Two major components are the conscious mind, the part of the mind that you think with, and the subconscious mind. The subconscious mind is a goal achieving mechanism that behaves much like a computer. A computer is given information, then responds to that information without judgement. For example, a bank employee programmed the bank's computer to take ten cents out of everyone's checking account and put it into his own. The computer made no value judgement. It didn't say

"Thou shalt not steal," or "Are you sure you want to do this? You may get caught." It just did what the programmer told it to do without judgement.

So it is with your subconscious mind. Every thought, every experience you have had is indelibly etched in the memory bank of your subconscious mind, never to be erased. The time you made the winning free throw in the big game, the time you starred in the high school musical, all of your successes are there. Unfortunately, so are the less pleasant incidents. The time you walked across your neighbor's lawn and got scolded, the time you made a fool of yourself at the school dance, the time you failed your Algebra II test. They are also etched in the memory bank of your subconscious mind.

If you feed yourself thoughts like, "I'm such a dummy," or "You never do anything right," your subconscious mind doesn't judge, it simply adds the information to its memory bank.

The workings of the human mind are so complicated and complex, and volumes have been written about its power, so one chapter of one book will not even scratch the surface of the available knowledge, but let's look at a few simple steps you can take to achieve mastery of your thoughts.

The first step, a theme we have emphasized often, is to create an awareness of what you are thinking and what you are doing. Awareness precedes change. Constantly monitor and adjust your thoughts. When you find yourself wallowing in negativity, carve it away and focus on something positive. Eckhart Tolle, in *The Power of Now*, suggests that when your mind is racing, quiet your inner dialogue by observing things around you: things like the beauty of nature or noticing a building that you have never noticed before, or marveling at the beautiful blend of colors on a billboard. Spend time daily in quiet meditation to calm your inner dialogue.

You can program your subconscious by use of positive affirmations, which is the topic of our next chapter. You can practice things we discuss in *How to Carve a Duck* one chapter at a time. At the top of the list, and perhaps the most difficult, is to assume total responsibility for the way you respond to the challenges you face. Resolve to keep your self-talk positive and strive to make love, peace, happiness, and harmony an expression of who you are.

CHAPTER 17

KEEPING YOUR SELF-TALK POSITIVE

What do you get when you squeeze an orange? Most people reply "orange juice," because that's what's inside of the orange. The same is true for us as human beings. When we get squeezed, what comes out is what's inside. If there is a lot of anger, bitterness, and frustration in your subconscious, under pressure, if left unchecked, it will manifest itself in hostile behavior. If, on the other hand, calmness and emotional intelligence have been programmed into the subconscious, the resulting response would be much different, at least most of the time.

Lew Tice, founder of the Pacific Institute, says that human beings are teleological in nature. Don't let the highfalutin term overwhelm you. All it means is that your words create pictures in the mind and your creative subconscious, aided by your imagination, helps move you towards completion of those pictures. Words are powerful. They can humiliate or humor, hurt or heal. They can create health and harmony, or they can create anger and bitterness.

Using that as our motivation, let's explore five tips for keeping self-talk positive. We will often use the term "affirmation," which by definition is "a statement asserting the existence or truth of something." Statements like "I am such a dummy" or "I never do anything right," repeated often enough, become "assertions of truth." Statements like "I am a kind and caring person" and "I talk to people in a calm and confident manner," have the same power as their negative counterparts, but produce dramatically different results.

The words that dominate your self-talk manifest in both behavior and emotional well-being. Recalling a concept from Chapter 16, your subconscious mind accepts and records your input without judgement, and as we have repeatedly said, "Be careful, because what you say is what you get."

Here are five tips for directing your affirmations towards the positive side of the ledger.

Tips for Writing Affirmations

A. **First Person – Present Tense.** Use phrases such as "I am" or "I have" or "I enjoy." This indicates that you already have the trait, and your creative subconscious will act accordingly. Phrases such as "I will" or "I am going to" will not elicit automatic response, although they may be a good interim step to start your thought process moving in a positive direction.

B. **Be Positive.** Your self-talk must paint pictures of your positive, wanted behavior. A statement such as "I am a patient loving parent. I talk to my kids in a calm, quiet, confident manner," will send those pictures to your subconscious. A statement such as "I don't want to scream and holler at my kids," will produce pictures of screaming and hollering and open the door to screaming and hollering.

C. **Do Not Compare Yourself to Others.** You are working to improve YOU. You are trying to become the best possible YOU, not trying to be better than someone else. A key to happy living is not to be better than anyone else, but to become better than your former self.

D. **Be Realistic.** Only affirm that which you can honestly see yourself achieving. If you're not athletically inclined, you are probably not going to make it as a center in the NBA. You could, however, become a super salesperson or a great teacher or a fantastic supervisor or secretary. Set your goals high but not out of sight. "Go as far as you can see. When you get there, you will be able to see further."

E. **Lock On—Lock Out.** Lock on to your positive thoughts and lock out all conflicting thoughts. The minute you feel doubting self-talk entering your mind, get rid of it and replace it with a reaffirmation of your positive aspirations. The process of positive self-talk will not work if you affirm positively part of the time but let doubting, conflicting, and negative thoughts dominate your thinking the rest of the time. Lock onto the positive and lock out all negatives, regardless of what may appear to be going on around you. Others may determine what *enters* your mind but you, and only you, determine what *stays* there.

EMOTIONAL INTELLIGENCE 101: *HOW TO CARVE A DUCK*

Let me illustrate the process by sharing my experience using Lew Tice's advice. Much of my authoritarian coaching style carried over into my parenting, which led to me screaming at my kids more than I wanted to. I had been telling myself, "I don't want to scream at my kids. I don't want to scream at my kids. I don't want to scream at my kids," but the picture I was painting of my behavior was screaming at my kids. In line with Lew's advice, I formulated this affirmation: "I am a patient loving father. I talk to my kids in a calm, quiet, and loving manner." I wrote the words on a 3x5 notecard, memorized it and repeated it often throughout the day. I would visualize and imagine my kids being upset and me staying calm and under control. Little by little I felt the change.

I started this in the mid-80s, and I would like to tell you that since then I have not once screamed at my kids. If you believe that, there's some ocean front property in Arizona I would like to talk to you about. This leads to review of tip #5, "Lock On –Lock Out." When you blow it, rather than give up or make an excuse, take a deep breath and reaffirm, "Hey, that's not like me. I am a patient, loving father. I talk to my kids in a calm, quiet and loving manner," and mentally rehearse handling the situation differently next time.

Whether you use your creative power to affirm achievement of "inside-of-you" goals like patience, confidence, or mastering your tone of voice or "outside-of-you" goals like a career goal or owning a lake home, it is important to pay attention to step #4, which is to be realistic. To determine whether a goal is realistic or not, determine who wins the argument between you and your "little twerps," those little inside voices. If they convince you that your goal is unachievable, redirect your expectations to something that you can fathom being within reach.

In the 90s, I was having coffee with a friend who said, "I could make $100,000 a year in this business." I asked, "Tom, do you believe that?" He said, "No." When asked if earning $50,000 was believable, he hedged a little bit. When I asked if he thought he could make $40,000, he didn't hesitate to say, "Yes." I suggested that he affirm that; to picture and visualize himself working hard enough and smart enough to earn $40,000, then moving up from there. Two years later he reached an income level of $100,000. The message is to break your goals into believable, doable chunks, adopt a "go as far as you can see and when you get there you will be able to see further" mentality. Then make it happen.

In our next chapter we are going to unite the power of positive self-talk with use of vivid imagination. For now, if the mood moves you, get a 3x5 card or a plain sheet of paper and practice writing affirmations that you can use to assist you in developing clarity, direction, and a sense of purpose for achievement of a goal or mastery of a personal trait. Carry it with you, and review it often.

Here are examples:

"I am a patient, loving person. I talk to people in a kind, soothing, and loving manner."

"I enjoy my self-confidence. I am comfortable meeting new people and making them feel relaxed being around me."

"Good is coming to me from all directions and I am open to receive it."

"I deal with upsetting situations in a calm and confident manner."

"The good I am seeking is now seeking me."

"The right and perfect job I am seeking is now seeking me."

"I accept things as they are for now."

"I have already let go of my anger towards _____."

"Just for today, I will not judge others. I accept people as they are and honor their miraculousness as human beings."

"I let go of the mistakes of the past and press on to even greater achievements of the future."*

"I promise myself that nothing will disturb my peace of mind."*

"I am to large for worry, to noble for anger, to strong for fear, and to happy to permit the presence of trouble."*

*Paraphrased from the "Optimist Creed," Optimist International.com.

CHAPTER 18

VIVID IMAGINATION

Picture a big juicy lemon in front of you. Now imagine cutting the lemon in half and taking a big bite. Taste the sour acidic juice as you pucker up in response. Take another huge bite and amplify the experience. Before you read on, close your eyes and vividly imagine this scenario.

After I do this exercise in my seminars, I ask the participants if any of them noticed increased salivation, and many of them do. The body's response to the taste of the sour lemon is to increase salivation, but the lemon existed only in the imagination. The subconscious mind often does not delineate between real and vividly imagined behavior. How many times have you felt anger build just thinking about the possibility of an upcoming confrontation? Have you felt joy just anticipating a reunion with a friend or family member? Emotions, even those triggered by thoughts, are experienced in the body. When you laugh, the body produces endorphins which result in a happy feeling. Through works of Norman Cousins, Candice Pert, and so many others, it has been scientifically documented to be true.

If thoughts and imagination are that powerful, why not choose to direct them towards positive outcomes? As you affirm and visualize yourself being happy and successful, your creative subconscious mind records the information as fact, and being "teleological" in nature, you are moved towards completion of the pictures you create. Notice the term "creative subconscious," and remember that it does create what you send it, both positive and negative, without judgment. Send it what you want it to create.

Action

Nothing happens without action, so let's create a partial list of things you can do to maximize the potential of self-talk and imagination.

1. Choose one or two traits or goals that you wish to bring to fruition and write affirmations describing the wanted results.
2. Write the affirmations on a card, carry it with you and repeat them often. When stopped in traffic, instead of getting uptight; relax, take a deep breath, quiet your mind, repeat your affirmations and enjoy the moment. Remember to visualize.
3. During your morning quiet time, tie your affirmations specifically to upcoming activities. If you are planning a business meeting, affirm that you are bringing warmth and enthusiasm to the meeting. Imagine (visualize) yourself being pleasant in the breakroom. Picture yourself weaving a warm smile into your daily conversions. Mentally rehearse being calm and patient in upsetting situations. In your imagination, redirect negative discussions towards a more positive focus.

4. Remembering that "Wherever You Go, There You Are," determine that today you are going to bring your best you wherever you go.
5. Do the same with your "outside of you" goals. Affirm, picture, and vividly imagine your desires unfolding in natural order, and lock out all conflicting thoughts.
6. One of the best tools for bringing your outside of you goals to fruition is fully live your inside of you goals.
7. Start your day and end your day on a positive note, using gratitude as a cornerstone. Your quiet time in the morning sets your direction for the day, and your positive reflection just before you drift off to sleep gives your creative subconscious hours to ruminate thoughts of love, happiness, harmony and success as you refresh yourself in slumber.

Keep Your Quiet Time Quite

Volumes have been written about the benefits of meditation and most prominent speakers and authors include it in their advice for stress-free living. The purpose is to clear your mind of the busy-ness and clutter that diminishes your focus, and to replace it with a calm serenity.

A couple of Buddhist monks shared some techniques that work for me. Get quiet and comfortable and focus on your breathing. Focus on the tip of your nose and gently quiet your mind. Feel your body relax as you enjoy the silence between the thoughts. If you wish, you can affirm something like "I am relaxed and at peace," then sit in silence. Take time every day to renew your spirituality and get in touch with the wonders of creation and your connection with it. We would be remiss if we didn't include paying attention to spiritual growth as an avenue to creating a fulfilling life.

This is nothing new – these messages have been around for literally thousands of years. It is up to each generation and to each of us individually to discover the power and absolute bliss that comes from the realization of our oneness with each other and with all of creation. Deepak Chopra in his *The Seven Spiritual Laws of Success* perhaps says it best:

> "We have stopped for a moment to encounter each other, to meet, to love, to share. This is a precious moment, but it is transient. It is a little parenthesis in eternity. If we share with caring, lightheartedness, and love, we will create abundance and joy for each other. And then this moment will have been worthwhile."

CHAPTER 19

PATIENCE

Patience is not an emotion; it's a decision.

A woman was stopped at a red light and when the light turned green her car stalled. A guy at the back of the line started blowing his horn and kept on blowing his horn and blowing his horn and blowing his horn. The woman got frustrated, walked back to his window and said, "Mister, if you would like to go up there and start my car for me, I would be glad to sit back here and blow your horn for you."

We've all been the guy blowing the horn, some of us more than others. We've all been impatient, some of us more often than others. Patience, like it's opposite, is learned and something anyone can master.

Thomas Harris wrote a book in the 60s entitled *I'm OK, You're OK* in which he outlined three behavioral responses to emotional situations.

Response #1 is that of the child.

I AM GOING TO ACT THE WAY I FEEL

A child gets upset, kicks his or her heels and throws a temper tantrum. The emotions are controlling the behavior. This is not limited to children. We are all capable of letting our emotional state dictate our behavior.

The second response is that of the parent.

<u>YOU</u> ARE GOING TO ACT THE WAY I FEEL

When my kids were growing up they might ask, "Dad, can we go to the park?" and I might say, "NO." When asked, "Why?" I might have answered, "Because I'm in a rotten mood, we can't go." Nine times out of 10 we would go, but because I was in a bad mood, they had to behave the way I felt.

This is not limited to parent/child relationships. We all have our days at work when we warn our co-workers, "I'm in a terrible mood. Just leave me alone."

A teacher had a rock on her desk that read on one side, "Teacher is in a good mood today." The other side informed the students, "Teacher is in a bad mood today." She created the expectation that they were to act the way she felt.

Neither of the responses are necessarily good nor bad, they just are. Anger isn't good nor bad, it just is. Emotions aren't good nor bad, they just are.

There is, however, a third response—that of the adult.

I CAN'T HELP THE WAY I FEEL RIGHT NOW, BUT I CAN CONTROL THE WAY I THINK AND ACT.

This is a beautiful patience affirmations. It's a fancy way of saying. "Count to ten before you do anything."

My wife was putting together a train set for our then

four-year-old grandson and things were not going smoothly. She said, "Dylan, I don't know if I can to this." He replied, "Gramma, take a deep breath, relax, and work very, very slowly." She had a high stress job as a clinic administrator at the time and said she couldn't count the number of times she would remind herself to take a deep breath, relax, and work very, very slowly.

You may wonder where a four-year-old got that idea. He and his father used to wrestle Ninja Warrior style. When they were done they would bow to each other, get into a Buddha-style meditative pose, close their eyes, and sit quietly for a minute or two. He discovered the transformative power of patience at age four.

We've all heard the prayer, "Lord grant me patience—right now." It doesn't happen that quickly, but with practice and resolve, increasing patience *is* possible. You can use the adult response in a variety of ways. In a stressful encounter with another person, silently use the words to calm yourself down and carve away impatience. During your quiet time, combine the words with visualization and pre-program calmness into your creative subconscious. The key component is desire. When your desire to remain controlled is greater than your willingness to fly off the handle, patience is the natural by-product just waiting to happen.

In Chapter 2, we defined emotional intelligence as "The ability to keep yourself under control, even when you don't want to." Patience and emotional intelligence go hand in hand.

EMOTIONAL INTELLIGENCE 101: *HOW TO CARVE A DUCK*

I CAN'T HELP THE WAY I FEEL RIGHT NOW, BUT I CAN CONTROL THE WAY I THINK AND ACT.

CHAPTER 20

DEALING WITH UPSET PEOPLE

On the subject of dealing with upset employees, a bank supervisor in one of my seminars said, "I kill 'em with kindness." When I asked what he meant by that he answered, "First, I get in step. I say something like, 'I'm really glad you came to see me about that, let's see what we can do to take care of it.'" That's a little different from the old authoritarian approach that would remind the employee of the number of people who would love their job, then remind them to not let the door hit their backside on the way out.

"Then I listen," which is a hard thing to do. We're all vaccinated with phonograph needles and we like to talk, talk, talk, but he said, "I just listen." Listening goes beyond planning what you are going to say when it's your turn; it means to truly tune in with empathy to what the other person has to say.

"Thirdly, we solve the problem." Solving the problem doesn't mean you have to say what the other person wants to hear. You have policies to uphold, you have others to think about, you have standards to adhere to, so meeting their expectations is not always possible. If you do a good job in steps one and two, however, your chances of them accepting your decisions are greatly increased.

One day I preceded my request for a favor from my principal by reminding him that I had volunteered mega hours working on a project for the district, thinking that would assure me of a favorable response. He said, "I have a lot of teachers who volunteer time, and if I let you do this, I would be obligated to grant the rest of them the same favor." It wasn't what I wanted to hear, but because we had always had open communications, I was willing to accept his decision.

He was a former English teacher and I taught math, so we had a lot of differences on grading philosophy and other issues, but we always had civil exchanges and I give him a lot of credit for his ability to model the three steps.

Like any of the skills we touch on, they are transferrable to your kids, your fellow service club members, your coworkers, your neighbors, or with anyone, and it starts, of course, with emotional intelligence. You become the soothing element that turns potential conflict into calm and constructive dialogue.

Anyone can fix the blame for a problem. Skilled leaders fix the problem.

Three Steps for Dealing with Upset People

- ➢ **Get in Step**
- ➢ **Listen**
- ➢ **Solve the Problem**

hours working on a project for the district, thinking that would assure me of a favorable response. He said, "I have a lot of teachers who volunteer time, and if I let you do this, I would be obligated to grant the rest of them the same favor." It wasn't what I wanted to hear, but because we had always had open communications, I was willing to accept his decision.

He was a former English teacher and I taught math, so we had a lot of differences on grading philosophy and other issues, but we always had civil exchanges and I give him a lot of credit for his ability to model the three steps.

Like any of the skills we touch on, they are transferrable to your kids, your fellow service club members, your coworkers, your neighbors, or with anyone, and it starts, of course, with emotional intelligence. You become the soothing element that turns potential conflict into calm and constructive dialogue.

Anyone can fix the blame for a problem. Skilled leaders fix the problem.

Three Steps for Dealing with Upset People

- ➢ **Get in Step**
- ➢ **Listen**
- ➢ **Solve the Problem**

CHAPTER 21

HOW CAN WE FIX THIS?

In my opinion, *My Fair Lady* is one of the most delightful musical comedies of all time. It was an honor to be cast in our local GREAT Theatre's production of the play and an even greater delight to learn from a phenomenal director. Her knowledge, enthusiasm, and love of theatre was just the tip of the iceberg. Her ability to teach, to lead, and to motivate was second only to her effectiveness in dealing with problems as they arose. She simply would ask, in her usual calm and upbeat tone of voice, "How can we fix this?"

What a skill set, and one that any of us can learn in a heartbeat. "How can we fix this?" You can use it at work, you can use it with your kids or your neighbors or anyone else for that matter. It can serve as a supervisory strategy as you confront problems with an individual staff member, or you can use it to set the stage for a brainstorming session with your entire team. Start by describing the situation you face, then pose the question, "How can we fix this?"

When the confrontation requires a more serious tone, simply modify your approach by saying, "We need to fix this," or "You need to fix this."

You can also use this to resolve situations that you may have created for yourself. "Hey, I really blew it and I'm sorry. How can we fix this?" or "What can I do to fix this?"

This idea is so simple and so easy we can fit it on one page. Just do it.

CHAPTER 22

THERE IS ANOTHER WAY

A little girl asked, "Mommy, why do you always cut off the ends of the ham?" The mother answered, "Well, I've always done it that way. That's what my mother taught me." So, the girl went to her grandmother and queried, "Gramma, how come you always cut of the ends of the ham?" "I've always done it that way," grandmother replied. "That's how my mother taught me to do it." When the little girl quizzed her great grandmother, Great Grandmother smiled and said, "My roaster was too short."

Often resistance to change comes from the fact that "we have always done it that way" or because we stand behind the "that's just the way I am" mentality. But to repeat what we said earlier, "If you always do what you've always done, you will always get what you always got." In other words, "If nothing changes, nothing changes."

A Lesson Learned

In my thirty plus years as a coach I got to know some good ones. One of the best was Bob Lateral, the sophomore basketball coach at Tech High School in St. Cloud, Minnesota. He said, "In my early days I was a screamer. I broke a lot of clip boards." One day his Athletic Director called him in and said "Bob, there is another way."

Taking that advice, Bob went to work on his coaching style and became one of the calmest coaches I have ever known. His teams were well-coached, well disciplined, well-organized, well-behaved, and they won. In fact, he won over 75% of his games as the sophomore coach at Tech. He was also the Girls' Softball Coach and won a couple of state championships along the way. He did it all without breaking clipboards.

The same was true in the classroom. He was mathematically sound, and you could hear a pin drop in the room. He achieved the same climate in his lower-level classes with students at risk as he did with his advanced students and did it all without raising his voice.

Do people who seem to always be in control of their emotional responses ever get angry? Of course they do, but they have learned to channel it constructively. Many times anger can motivate us to get things done or to work for necessary change, so the challenge is to master the response. Aristotle said it best:

> **Anyone can get angry – that is easy; but to be angry with the right person, and to the right degree, and at the right time, and for the right purpose, and in the right way – that is not within everyone's power and is not easy.**

The phrase "not within everyone's power" poses a good question. It may not be achievable for everyone, but is it achievable for *YOU?*" That can only be answered by you, but I firmly believe that with determination and practice, almost everyone can become a master of self-control.

An important consideration here is that very few components of emotional intelligence are "one and done," but an everyday challenge, so stick with it. Stay aware of your awareness, monitor and adjust as needed, guide yourself back on course when necessary, and give yourself a pat on the back for your progress. You can achieve anything you want to achieve without breaking clip boards.

CHAPTER 23

THE NATURAL ORDER OF THINGS

A plane takes off from Minneapolis destined for San Francisco. As it flies over Omaha, the Minneapolis control tower radios that the plane is off course, so the pilot turns around and heads back to Minneapolis to start over, right? Of course not. The pilot makes a slight adjustment and gets back on course.

The same is true in almost any phase of your life. You have a destination in mind, but invariably things don't always go according to Hoyle. A friend of mine defines life as that which happens while you are making other plans. That doesn't mean your plans are not good and not worth pursuing, it is simply an indication that ups and downs are what life is all about. To paraphrase advice from Peanuts character Linus Van Pelt, "There is always crab grass in the lawn of life."

When things get off course, apply the analogy of the plane trip from Minneapolis to San Francisco. Make an adjustment and get back on course. If you need to get on the pity pot for a little while, do so, but keep it short.

Love, peace and harmony are the natural order of things. This is true of your family life, your relationships, your career, and all phases of existence. That affirmation is not meant to present a Pollyannaish approach to the ebb and flow of life, but to serve as a track to run on; a course to return to when things seem out of whack.

When events seem to be in turmoil, carve away what you can and intelligently deal with what you can't. Temper that with a knowing that there may be things that won't change *for now,* but options may become apparent down the road.

Achieving serenity and peace of mind may require letting go of anger or forgiving a grudge. It might mean coaching yourself to be less upsettable or eliminating negative self-talk or ceasing to berate yourself. You are the one piloting the plane, so you get to determine what adjustments are made on the journey. You're the one carving the duck.

Whether you think you deserve or not, it is the intention of the Universe for you to live a rich, full, happy life. Convince yourself that you *are* deserving. Cast aside your fear and doubt and know that "Love, peace and harmony are the natural order of things."

Love, peace, and harmony are the natural order of things.

CHAPTER 24

GET OUT OF JUDGEMENT

If you want to make others happy, show compassion. If you want to make yourself happy, show compassion. An ultimate level of compassion can be demonstrated by getting out of judgment and accepting people and circumstances as they are.

It's the Second Thought That Counts.

People who say they don't judge others lie about other things too, so let's put this in perspective. We constantly and instantaneously judge others. So, it's not the first thought, but the second thought that counts. When you realize that your initial thought was judgmental, you have the power to alter it immediately.

A spiritual leader 2000 years ago admonished us to "Judge not by appearance, but by righteous judgment." Let's illustrate. You're walking down the street and see an unkempt homeless person approaching. You may initially notice the shaggy hair, the scraggly beard, the ragged coat, and your first thought might be, "How will he ever get a job looking like that?" But then you catch your judgmental thought and realize that you are about to encounter another human being who is deserving of your love and respect. You make eye contact, smile, and say, "Good Morning."

How do you think he feels? Not many acknowledge him,

let alone give him a smile and a warm greeting. But you did, and he probably feels pretty good.

Here's the kicker. How do you feel? Your love, your kindness, and your realization of the miraculousness of another human being elevated your consciousness to the highest level, and you're feeling pretty warm and fuzzy. You indeed became the biggest beneficiary of your kindness.

So when you detect a racist or a sexist or a judgmental thought about another's socio-economic status, gently forgive yourself and remind yourself that it's the second thought that counts. Then turn your attention to becoming accepting of the other person just the way he or she is.

This is analogous to an electric cord. The cord doesn't produce electricity, it merely conducts it, and when it does it gets warm. You and I are maybe not the source of this Divine thing we call love, but we conduct it, and when we do, like the electric cord, we get warm. Take advantage of every opportunity to be a conductor. In fact, work towards becoming a super conductor.

Pope John Paul II issued this challenge: "Society as a whole must respect, defend, and promote the dignity of every human person, at every moment, and in every condition of that person's life."

Notice it ends with a period. It doesn't have a comma then go on to say, "Unless he or she is a different race, a different religion, a different socio-economic status, a different sexual orientation, or dresses differently than me. It says *every* human person, at *every* moment, and in *every* condition of that person's life." That's a tall order for any organization, any community, any school, or even for you and me individually to live up to. But if we do, we can put an end to the racism, sexism and other forms of hatred and discrimination that exist in America and in the world. When enough of us do that, we will bring the rest along.

CHAPTER 25

LIGHT A SINGLE CANDLE

Father Keller founded the Christopher organization in America and he used as their motto, "It is better to light a single candle than to curse the darkness." To illustrate the dynamics of his message, while preaching at Notre Dame Stadium one night he turned off all the lights and the stadium was dark.

He lit a single candle and the light from that one candle pierced the darkness. Then he started to light the candles of the people around him and they started to light the candles of the people around them, and soon the once darkened stadium was aglow with light, simply because he lit one single candle.

You never know where the light from your candle is going to stop. When I was a student at St. Cloud State I was traveling down to my hometown of Morton to celebrate my Dad's 65th birthday. About ten miles from town my car conked out. I know a lot about cars—some are green, some are blue. I had no idea what to do.

I walked to a farmhouse about a quarter mile away and the farmer came out, tinkered under the hood for a few minutes and said, "Try it now." I did and the car started. He walked past my window and I sheepishly said, "Gee, I don't have any cash, but I would be glad to write you a check." He answered, "Don't worry about that. We all have to help each other out along the way." Those words hit me. "We all have to help each other out along the way."

Because of that time, I can't count the number of times I have stopped to help a stranded motorist because at one time, he lit one single candle. And who knows, maybe somebody that I stopped to helped stopped to help somebody else and they stopped to help somebody else. Maybe right now somewhere in the world, one person is getting help from another person simply because at one point in time, over fifty years ago, he lit one single candle.

As we near conclusion of *How to Carve a Duck,* I leave you with this challenge for today, tomorrow, and every single day of your life.

Is there anyone that's happier
Because you passed their way?
Is there someone who remembers
That you spoke to them today?

Was your day a day of progress,
Was it well or sorely spent?
Did you leave a trail of kindness?
Or scars of discontent?

Did you really make the most of
This day that slipped by fast?
Did you help one single person
Of the many that you passed?

When today is almost over,
And its toiling time is through,
Is there just one person then
To say a kindly word of you?

And as you close your eyes in slumber,
Do you think that God will say?
"You deserve one more tomorrow
For the good you did today.

CHAPTER 26

THE BEGINNING

It is my hope that *How to Carve a Duck* doesn't end here, but merely finds a new beginning. The ideas shared have maximum impact when you review them often and put them into practice. Revisit the chapters most meaningful to you and benefit from the power of spaced repetition. Like the skills of the free throw shooter or the golfer, mastery requires practice and determination.

The format is intentional—to provide small doses of inspiration that can be read, digested, and put into focus one idea at a time. It is meant to make it easy to bring thoughts and ideas to the forefront of your thinking because, to repeat for the third or fourth time, "You become what you think about most of the time."

Self-help books are available by the thousands and there is a reason for that. Learning to stay calm under fire, to be more patient, to practice forgiveness and to deal calmly with upset people takes time, determination, and repetition. About the time you think you have let go of something that happened in the past, it reappears, so you have to let go all over again. None of these things are one and done. Problems keep resurfacing and mastery takes vigilance. Every day brings new challenges and with them, new opportunities to test your positivity. So prepare yourself daily to answer the call. If you want to keep chopping, you have to sharpen the ax.

What's Important to You

In the introduction, we suggested a number of ways to use *How to Carve a Duck*. You can go back to the "Carve Your Own Duck" assessment on page three, prioritize one or two items from the list and commit to work on those for the next six months. Find the chapter or chapters that provide the information and inspiration you need and set things in motion.

You may randomly select a page and find that it's just what the doctor ordered—your prescription for optimism as you engage in the activities of the day.

If you are dealing with a problem, a few minutes reviewing "Solution Consciousness" may be time well spent. Chapter 23 on "The Natural Order of Things" may be just what you need to inject a shot of **P**ositive **M**ental **A**ttitude into your day. The idea of using this or any book as a reference is to refresh your mind on a regular basis.

I should. I can. I will.

We close many seminars with an exercise to formulate an action plan, so let's do the same here. Choose just one or two skills that you want to hone and resolve to make them a priority for the next several months. Then make a commitment to work on them until they become habit. Tell yourself, "I *should* be more confident. I *can* be more confident. I *will* be more confident." or "I *should* learn to be more relaxed." I *can* learn to be more relaxed. I *will* learn to be more relaxed."

Take a minute to write a note to yourself:

I should_____

I can_____

I will_____

Realize that moving from "I should" to "I will" may take a year to register, illustrating that growth is often times slow and incremental, but stick with it and it will happen. You can write your "I should, I can, and I will" pledge on a card and carry it with you.

To reflect on something we shared in the opening chapter, just as the perfect duck exists within the block of wood waiting for the skilled artist to reveal it, the perfect you already exists within you, ready to manifest a life of success, happiness, prosperity, and laughter. That is indeed a wonderful thought and something you can run with.

EMOTIONAL INTELLIGENCE 101: *HOW TO CARVE A DUCK*

Summary

Dr. Jerald Jampolsky's *Love is Letting Go of Fear,* was just over 100 pages with a lot of illustrations. I thought, "Boy, Jerry, you pulled one over on us, there's not a lot of text here." But the book added so much to my life and I loved the format. It was short, precise, and easy to read, so I decided that if I were ever to write a book, it would be short, precise, and easy to read. With that in mind, *How to Carve a Duck* is a potpourri of short vignettes meant to serve up small doses of inspiration, one thought at a time.

There is a line in Frank Sinatra's retirement song, *I Did it My Way*, that sums up my motivation for writing *How to Carve a Duck:* "Regrets, I've had a few, but then again, too few to mention." My biggest regret is that to many times my lack of self-control prevented me from being all that I could be. I wrote this to encourage you, the reader, to replace the "my way or the highway" mentality with time tested self-coaching tools that foster more patience, more confidence, an ability to solve problems in a calm manner, and to use a more controlled and approachable tone of voice.

The trek is exciting at any age, but I especially encourage young people to pay attention to these things as early in life as possible. Don't wait–Do it now. To you more seasoned readers, I remind you again that it is never too late to learn. Growth at our age is gratifying and a fountain of youth.

Make a decision to get as much kick out of life as possible and to live in a state of happiness most of the time. Life is a banquet. Why bring a sandwich?

About the Author

Denny Smith is a former teacher and coach and a high energy speaker with a singular mission: To build peoples' confidence, to increase peoples' competence and help people get a bigger kick out of life, both on and off the job. His sometimes emotional, sometimes humorous, but always sincere approach to his audience and subject matter has been enjoyed by business groups, sales organizations, health care professionals, educators, and students in 21 states and Canada. He is a teacher, an author, a motivator, and a skill builder.

Made in the USA
Columbia, SC
19 May 2021